Michael and Jane Pelusey
THE MEDIA
Magazines

CHELSEA HOUSE
PUBLISHERS
A Haights Cross Communications Company ®
Philadelphia

Chelsea House Publishers
2080 Cabot Boulevard West, Suite 201
Langhorne, PA 19047-1813

The Chelsea House world wide web address is www.chelseahouse.com

First published in 2005 by
MACMILLAN EDUCATION AUSTRALIA PTY LTD
627 Chapel Street, South Yarra 3141

Visit our website at www.macmillan.com.au

Associated companies and representatives throughout the world.

Library of Congress Cataloging-in-Publication Data applied for.
ISBN 0 7910 8804 9

Edited by Anne Löhnberg and Angelique Campbell-Muir
Text and cover design by Ivan Finnegan, iF Design
All photographs and images used in design © Pelusey Photography.
Cover photograph: Magazine editor, courtesy of Pelusey Photography.

Printed in China

Acknowledgments

Michael and Jane Pelusey would like to thank *Homes and Living Magazine* and *XPress Magazine* for their assistance.
The publisher is grateful to the following for permission to reproduce copyright material:

All photographs courtesy of Pelusey Photography.

While every care has been taken to trace and acknowledge copyright, the publisher tenders their apologies for any accidental infringement where copyright has proved untraceable. Where the attempt has been unsuccessful, the publisher welcomes information that would redress the situation.

CONTENTS

When a word is printed in bold, you can look up its meaning in the glossary on page 31.

THE MEDIA

People communicate in many different ways. One thing common to all forms of communication is that a message is conveyed. Communicating is about spreading information and sharing it with others, in spoken and written words as well as in pictures.

The different means we use to communicate are called media. Each of them is designed to spread information and news, entertain people, or let them share experiences. The audience can be one person or a million. Forms of communication that reach millions of people at the same time are called mass media. They include:

◎   magazines
◎   film and television
◎   the Internet
◎   newspapers
◎   photography
◎   radio.

The media have great influence in our everyday lives. They inform us about current events, expose us to advertising, and entertain us.

Media play an important role in a family's life.

Hundreds of magazines are published every week.

MAGAZINES

Magazines are popular reading material. They form an important source of communication and entertainment.

The word *magazine* comes from the French word for "department store," *magasin*. Just as department stores are full of different goods to meet people's needs, magazines cover a huge range of topics. There are magazines for all age groups and both **genders**. They cover most hobbies and interests.

In our busy world, people read magazines to relax. They are a popular alternative to a newspaper or book. The articles in a magazine take less time to read than a book, and the format makes it easy for people to browse and read snippets of information.

Magazines differ from newspapers in their style of printing and in the types of stories they present. Magazine paper is often **glossy**, and the printing is usually in full-color.

Articles in magazines are often longer and more in-depth than stories in newspapers. On the other hand, daily newspapers offer more up-to-date news, because they come out more frequently. Magazines are printed weekly, monthly, every two months, twice a year, or sometimes just once a year.

EARLY MAGAZINES

Magazines have changed dramatically over the last 300 years. They evolved as the technologies and the attitudes in society changed.

The Review was probably the first magazine in Britain. It was published in the early 1700s and written by Daniel Defoe (who also wrote the novel *Robinson Crusoe*). Later, *Tattler* and *Spectator* followed. The difference between newspapers and magazines at this stage was that newspapers published news, while magazines published people's opinions.

Advertisements in a magazine from the 1950s

More readers

Originally, magazines were designed for the rich and well-educated. As more and more people learned to read, publishers dropped the price of

National Geographic has been published since 1888; *LIFE* since 1936.

magazines so more people would buy them. Businesses soon realized that by advertising in magazines, they could tell many people about their products and services.

Pictures

The introduction of pictures changed the **layout** of magazines. At first, each picture had to be etched into wood or metal so it could be printed in the magazine. Sketchers were sent to events to capture the scene.

Better printing

In the 1900s, the printing quality of magazines became much better. As printing techniques improved, photos were added: first in black and white and later in color. By the 1950s, magazines had developed into the glossy full-color publications with many photos that we know today.

More creative design

The use of **digital** technology allows designers to create images that were impossible before. This has led to greater creative freedom in magazine design, particularly on front covers. The front cover must dazzle viewers, to tempt them to pick up the magazine off the shelf and buy it.

Changed attitudes

As opinions in society have changed, so have magazines. Women's magazines once were all about recipes and home-making ideas. These topics are still covered today, but over the last 30 years, women's magazines have developed to include subjects such as women's rights, relationships, and **issues** for working mothers.

NEWS FLASH

FAMOUS MAGAZINES
Vanity Fair
National Geographic
LIFE
Women's Weekly
Vogue
Harper's
Sports Illustrated

Women's magazines

TYPES OF MAGAZINES

Each magazine has its own **target audience**. This includes age, interest, occupations, education, and income. Some magazines are aimed specifically at men or women, while many others are interesting to both genders.

Women's magazines

Magazines for women are the largest category of magazines. The publishers and advertisers gather information about what certain groups of women like. This affects the writing style and which products are advertised.

Married women with children often like to read about home decorating, cooking, travel, and famous people. Younger single women may read about relationships, personal stories, and activities for young people.

Cooking magazines, showing beautiful pictures of food, are aimed mostly at women.

Men's magazines

Men's magazines are relatively new. They cover topics such as male fitness and health. Magazines about cars, boats, fishing, and sports are also read mostly by men, although plenty of women enjoy reading them, too.

Current affairs magazines

Current affairs magazines publish articles about local and global events of that week or month. The stories are similar to those in newspapers, but cover the subjects in more depth.

Most readers of fishing magazines are men.

Special-interest magazines

Special-interest magazines cover one topic in great detail. There are thousands of special-interest magazines, writing about all the different things people are interested in.

SPORTS MAGAZINES

There are many magazines for people who like to play or watch sports. Some cover all sports; others focus on one particular sport, such as football and baseball.

There are also magazines about leisure activities such as kayaking and hiking. They are read by people who do the activity and by people who would like to. They publish articles about equipment and places to go, and interviews with experts at the activity.

LIFESTYLE MAGAZINES

Magazines about cooking, decorating, home repairs, and travel are called lifestyle magazines. The articles tell people how they can improve the way they live.

Trade magazines

Some magazines, known as **trade** magazines, are not for sale to the general public. They meet the specialized needs of people in a particular line of work, such as medicine or engineering.

Sports magazines

Lifestyle magazines

WORKING ON MAGAZINES

Each magazine is created by a number of people, all of whom have different talents and training.

The editor

The editor makes the decisions about what goes into every **issue** of the magazine. He or she coordinates all the articles coming into the office.

For magazines with a big **circulation**, the editor's job is often shared. There can be separate editors who are in charge of the fashion,

The editor decides which articles will appear in the magazine.

travel, and food sections. For small magazines with fewer staff, the editor often has other duties as well, such as writing articles.

Journalists

Journalists find interesting stories, interview people, and write articles for the magazine. Journalists are skilled at investigating topics and writing informative articles. Some journalists write their articles from home and sell them to different magazines for publication. These people are **freelance** journalists. If a magazine buys articles from freelance journalists, it does not need to have a big staff. It can also choose articles about a wide range of topics.

A journalist writes an article on her computer.

Photographers

Experienced photographers take photographs to accompany the articles in the magazine. Like journalists, they can be freelance or part of the magazine's staff. Other photographers take photos of products that are shown in advertisements.

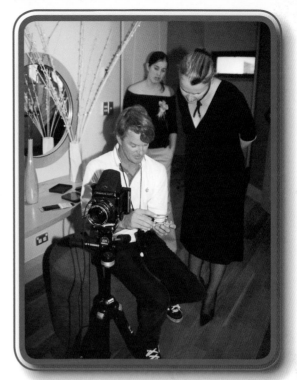

A photographer takes photographs on location for a lifestyle magazine.

The advertising staff

Advertisements bring in money, so the price of the magazine can stay low. The advertising staff sells space for advertisements in the magazine to businesses that want to promote their products. Usually, they call up companies and encourage them to advertise in the magazine. Some magazines print articles that promote a product. Because they are part advertisement and part **editorial**, these articles are called *advertorials*.

The graphic designer

The graphic designer takes all the articles, photographs, and advertisements and uses the computer to create an attractive layout. The most important page of a magazine is the front cover. The graphic designer places images and text on the front cover in such a way that they will catch people's eye in stores.

A graphic designer creates the cover for a music magazine.

FROM IDEA TO MAGAZINE

Every magazine article begins with an idea. This is the first stage in creating a complete magazine. After the ideas have been developed, there are several other important stages to go through before the magazine is published. The stages on the flow chart below show how magazines are created.

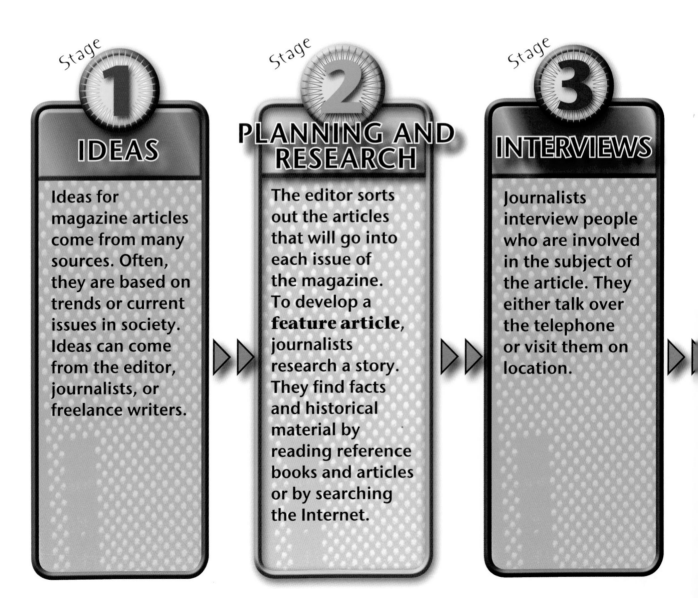

Stage
1
IDEAS

Ideas for magazine articles come from many sources. Often, they are based on trends or current issues in society. Ideas can come from the editor, journalists, or freelance writers.

Stage
2
PLANNING AND RESEARCH

The editor sorts out the articles that will go into each issue of the magazine. To develop a **feature article**, journalists research a story. They find facts and historical material by reading reference books and articles or by searching the Internet.

Stage
3
INTERVIEWS

Journalists interview people who are involved in the subject of the article. They either talk over the telephone or visit them on location.

Magazine case studies

Read the six stages from idea to magazine on pages 14–23 for three different magazine case studies:

CASE STUDY 1
A four-wheel drive magazine

CASE STUDY 2
A home and lifestyle magazine

CASE STUDY 3
A music magazine

A photographer on location

Stage **4**

WRITING

With all their research material and interview notes at hand, the journalists write their articles. They can include detailed descriptions of events, personal opinions, and **profiles** of interesting people.

Stage **5**

PHOTOGRAPHS

Often, photographers are assigned to take photographs to illustrate the articles. Sometimes the editor or journalist selects photographs that have already been taken.

Stage **6**

EDITING, LAYOUT AND PRINTING

The articles are **edited** to fit the magazine's format. Spelling, facts, and grammar are checked. Then the designer puts the articles, photographs, and advertising together to create an attractive magazine. The magazines are printed and **distributed**.

13

1 IDEAS

Ideas for articles can come from many places or sources. It is the editor's responsibility to choose articles that will interest the readers of the magazine. The ideas are discussed and finalized at an editorial meeting.

Stage

1 CASE STUDY 1

A FOUR-WHEEL DRIVE MAGAZINE

Pat, the editor of an adventure magazine, sifts through a mountain of ideas from his staff and from freelance writers each month. Companies also send in details of new products to be reviewed.

The magazine publishes articles about off-road driving.

Stage

1 CASE STUDY 2

A HOME AND LIFESTYLE MAGAZINE

For this lifestyle magazine, builders and architects send in information about their work. New ideas for decoration and garden designs are welcome. The editor and journalists meet to discuss the next issue of the magazine. They will run an article on the design and decorating of a new home.

Stage

1 CASE STUDY 3

A MUSIC MAGAZINE

The editorial staff of a weekly music magazine meets to discuss ideas about music and entertainment. They find out which artists will be on tour soon and consider interviewing them for a profile story. They also **review** new CDs.

PLANNING AND RESEARCH

The articles in each issue of the magazine need to fit together. Often, the editor chooses a range of articles with a common theme. Then journalists set out to prepare their articles.

CASE STUDY 1

A FOUR-WHEEL DRIVE MAGAZINE

Pat plans each issue months in advance. He chooses stories on new or modified cars, new products, and vacation destinations. Pat asks Rick, a freelance journalist, to write a story about a modified four-wheel-drive camper. Rick arranges to meet with the owner of the camper.

CASE STUDY 2

A HOME AND LIFESTYLE MAGAZINE

The magazine contains unique articles, but also monthly sections on gardening, renovations, and new homes. If the editor has too many articles about gardens, she holds some for the next issue. Hayley, a journalist, will interview the interior designer at the new house. She looks up information about other work by this designer.

The editor and Hayley discuss the style of the feature with a photographer.

The editor asks Natalie to write an article.

CASE STUDY 3

A MUSIC MAGAZINE

A famous musician is coming on a concert tour. Natalie, a journalist, finds out the tour dates and does research on the artist. She uses **press releases** and the Internet as sources of information.

3 INTERVIEWS

Interviews involve talking with people who are knowledgeable about a subject or product. Interviews can be done in person or over the telephone. Usually, the journalist takes notes, or records the conversation with a small recorder.

Stage

3

CASE STUDY 1

A FOUR-WHEEL DRIVE MAGAZINE

Rick talks to the owner of the modified four-wheel-drive camper and asks him for technical information. He also test-drives the camper, so he can give the readers his own opinion. The test drive is done in a beautiful area, so the photographer can take good photos. The location may also be the basis of another article. Readers interested in modifying their own vehicles will find the information in this article very useful.

ROLLAVAN

TOY BOX

Rick takes the camper for a test drive on a rough track.

Hayley (left) interviews the interior designer in the new house.

CASE STUDY 2

A HOME AND LIFESTYLE MAGAZINE

The interior designer, Kim, is eager to meet Hayley at the house. The interview will be good publicity for her. Later, Hayley will also talk to the owner of the house and the architect who designed it. Hayley has prepared questions to ask Kim. Depending on the answers, other questions may lead the interview in another direction.

CASE STUDY 3

A MUSIC MAGAZINE

Natalie calls the musician's manager and arranges a time to schedule an interview. Because the musician is in another country, the difference in time zones needs to be taken into consideration. Famous musicians can be difficult to interview, because they are very busy and meet lots of journalists. Natalie tries to ask questions that no one may have asked before.

Natalie does her interview over the phone.

17

4 WRITING

Most feature articles for magazines have roughly the same structure. They start with a headline that summarizes the subject. A subheading gives a brief description in one or two sentences. The first paragraph of the article should be catchy, so the readers keep reading. The main text is divided into paragraphs that flow from one to the next. A summary finishes off the article.

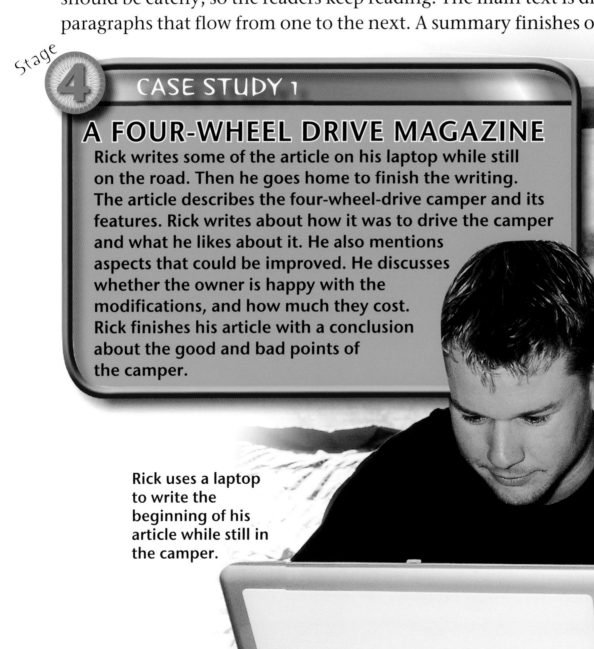

Stage

4

CASE STUDY 1

A FOUR-WHEEL DRIVE MAGAZINE

Rick writes some of the article on his laptop while still on the road. Then he goes home to finish the writing. The article describes the four-wheel-drive camper and its features. Rick writes about how it was to drive the camper and what he likes about it. He also mentions aspects that could be improved. He discusses whether the owner is happy with the modifications, and how much they cost. Rick finishes his article with a conclusion about the good and bad points of the camper.

Rick uses a laptop to write the beginning of his article while still in the camper.

Stage

4 CASE STUDY 2

A HOME AND LIFESTYLE MAGAZINE

Hayley gathers all her information and begins to write the article. She describes the home in detail and uses lots of **quotes** from the designers. They explain the reasons for special features in the house. Homes are very personal, so Hayley also includes in her article the owner's thoughts about the house.

Hayley writes the article on her computer at work.

Stage

4 CASE STUDY 3

A MUSIC MAGAZINE

Natalie writes her article about the musician, choosing words and a writing style that suit his fans. She writes about his music style and career and gives details about his touring schedule. She discusses his recent CDs and past concerts. She also gives an idea of his personality and what it was like to talk to him.

Natalie uses ideas from a CD cover to write her article.

5 PHOTOGRAPHS

Photographs illustrate most feature articles. Good quality, eye-catching images are required in glossy magazines.

Stage

5

CASE STUDY 1

A FOUR-WHEEL DRIVE MAGAZINE

The photographer's job is to take photographs of the camper for the article. A special location is chosen for the photographs, so that they give the article visual impact. The photographer takes pictures of the camper as a whole and of its details, such as the seats, dashboard, and engine. He also captures images of the camper driving along a rugged track, to show the reader what it can do. Many photos are taken, but only about six will be used in the magazine. The editor chooses the ones that best illustrate the article.

The camper in a scenic spot

CASE STUDY 2

A HOME AND LIFESTYLE MAGAZINE

Taking photos of buildings is a specialist field. Damien is an architectural photographer who works freelance for the magazine. He sets up special lights to brighten the indoor areas evenly. Architectural photographers use a camera on a **tripod** for this kind of work.

Damien carefully picks the angles, to photograph the best features of the home. He takes some pictures that show Hayley and the designer in the house as well.

Damien takes photographs at the house. The "umbrella" on the left produces even light.

CASE STUDY 3

A MUSIC MAGAZINE

There is no opportunity to take photographs for the music magazine article, because the article will be published before the musician arrives on his tour. Natalie requests some photographs from the musician's manager. Digital images can be e-mailed around the world in minutes. When the photos arrive, Natalie picks two that work with her article. The photographer can also take photographs at the concert for the follow-up article if needed.

Digital photos of pop stars and bands are available on the computer.

6 EDITING, LAYOUT, AND PRINTING

The editor makes sure all articles are well-written and the spelling and grammar are correct. Then a graphic designer lays out the finished articles, photographs, and advertising to fit the magazine's design. When the magazine is complete, it is digitally sent to the printer. The pages are printed, bound into magazines, and distributed to stores.

The final article about the four-wheel-drive camper

CASE STUDY 1

A FOUR-WHEEL DRIVE MAGAZINE

Once the journalists have finished writing all the articles, Pat and the **subeditor** read through them and edit them. Because each article has been given a certain amount of space in the magazine, each must be a fixed number of words or it won't fit. Rick's article should be 1,500 words. If it is longer than that, the subeditor will cut words out. The graphic designer arranges the articles, photographs, and advertisements on the computer into the format the readers will see in the finished magazine.

Graphic designer Sarah does the layout for the home design magazine.

CASE STUDY 2

A HOME AND LIFESTYLE MAGAZINE

When Hayley finishes her article, she e-mails it to Clare, the editor. Clare edits the article, checking the facts and the language. The edited text and the photographs taken by Damien are given to Sarah, the graphic designer. Sarah arranges the words and photos into an article. She prints a copy of the laid-out article, and Clare and another journalist **proofread** it for errors. The finished articles are sent to the printer. Clare receives a final print-out of the entire magazine for a last check. The magazine is then printed on glossy paper, ready for distribution.

CASE STUDY 3

A MUSIC MAGAZINE

Natalie's interview is added to the other feature articles for the music magazine. They are combined with the film and CD reviews and a guide to music shows to complete the magazine. The articles are edited and photographs chosen. The graphic designer puts them all together. Then the magazine is printed, and boxes full of magazines are ready to be sent to newsstands and readers.

The graphic designer looks at front pages of past issues of the music magazine.

DELIVERING THE MESSAGE

Magazines are a major way to communicate and to entertain people. Once they are printed, the magazines are packaged into large parcels and distributed around the country and the world. Magazines are available to their readers in many ways.

At shops and newsstands

Many shops and stalls sell magazines and newspapers. Most newsstands sell a huge range of magazines on many different subjects.

By subscription

Most magazines are available by **subscription**. The reader pays the magazine company for a whole year's worth of magazines. Each issue then arrives in the mail, usually before it is available at the shops. Often, the magazine is wrapped in plastic to protect it in the mailbox.

A store owner scans the price of a magazine.

A subscription is usually cheaper than buying each issue of the magazine separately. The publisher gives a discount, because the sale is guaranteed for a year. Some people subscribe to magazines that come from other countries and are not available locally. They may have to pay more, because of shipping costs.

All of these magazines are available by subscription.

In libraries

Many libraries have magazines for loan, just like library books. The library buys the magazines. You can take older issues home with you, but the most recent issues must stay in the library so everyone can read them.

Trade magazines in the library

Through clubs

Many people become members of a club or organization because they are interested in a specific subject, such as bird-watching. Their membership includes a copy of the club's magazine. It may be a simple newsletter or a glossy magazine with many pages. The magazine is sent to the members through the mail.

Through professional organizations

People who all work in the same type of job—such as nurses, doctors, or accountants—often join a professional organization that represents them. The membership usually includes a trade magazine, which contains articles about changes and developments as well as other news in their line of work. These magazines are not for sale to the general public.

Members of a bird-watching club receive a magazine every two months.

CAREERS IN MAGAZINES

Many people work in the magazine industry. Many have had formal college educations. Others learn their work on the job.

Clare is an editor

Clare is the editor of a lifestyle magazine.

"I worked in another field before studying journalism at college. After college, I got a job at this magazine as a journalist. I then became the deputy editor and later the editor. Although it is a very busy job, I like meeting new people and seeing homes being built or renovated."

Hayley is a journalist

Hayley is a journalist and enjoys traveling.

"I studied journalism and Indonesian at college. It was a great course. Afterward, I got a job working for a travel magazine based in Asia. I travel regularly throughout Asia, particularly Indonesia because I can speak the language. When I am back home, I work on a casual basis for other magazines, such as this lifestyle magazine."

Glen owns a newsstand

" After years in another profession, I wanted a complete change. So I bought a newsstand. I get to meet lots of people, and I enjoy reading magazines. "

Glen straightens the magazines at his newsstand.

Sarah is a graphic designer

" To have a career in graphic design, I studied design at college. I gained experience in advertising and publishing before I found this job. I like the creative side to designing magazine layout, using color and images. "

Sarah designs pages for the lifestyle magazine.

Damien is a photographer

" I did a diploma course in photography. I then worked as assistant to a professional photographer. With the experience I gained, I started my own business. Now I do magazine, commercial, and portrait photography. "

Damien concentrates hard when he takes a photograph.

MAGAZINES IN SOCIETY

Magazines are popular around the world. Millions of copies are sold every week in many languages.

Trends and fashion

Magazines keep people aware of what is popular. The fashion industry uses magazines to publicize the newest looks in clothes, hair design, and makeup. The long time between planning a magazine and it reaching the shelves means that photographs of new summer fashions, must often be taken in the middle of winter. Sometimes the models and photographers go to tropical islands for the photo shoot.

Models in fashion magazines

Most models in magazines are much thinner than ordinary people. This could contribute to eating disorders, because it raises unrealistic expectations, especially among young people.

Information

Feature articles in magazines can inform us about the world. We can use magazine articles to research vacation locations, design a garden, or learn about conditions in another country.

The subjects in magazines are controlled by the editors. Some people wonder whether the content in a magazine is sometimes changed to keep the big advertisers happy. In that case, readers may not get a true picture of what is happening.

A range of travel magazines to plan a vacation

Entertainment

Many magazines are designed to entertain us. That is why the waiting rooms of dentists, doctors, and mechanics have piles of magazines for clients to read. While they are waiting, people relax by reading magazines.

Some companies publish magazines especially for people to read while they are waiting. The clients at a hair salon can browse through magazines showing current hair designs, and perhaps decide on a new hairstyle.

Celebrity

Our society is fascinated by how rich and famous people go about their everyday lives. Many magazines cover this subject and nothing else.

Photographers called **paparazzi** keep a lookout for celebrities who are on vacation or dining at restaurants. These photographers are often accused of invading people's privacy. Articles are written about the celebrities, sometimes based on untrue rumors about their lives. On the other hand, the same stars may use these magazines to promote their next movie or CD.

Celebrity magazines

THE FUTURE OF MAGAZINES

Magazines have changed since they were first invented, and they will continue to change as society changes.

Competition on the Internet

Millions of people are turning to the Internet for entertainment and information. Magazine publishing companies are concerned that people spend time on the Internet instead of buying and reading their products. They are now producing **online** versions of their magazines, called electronic magazines, or e-zines. These can offer more variety to the reader, such as video clips and articles from past issues. The publisher may only offer some of the articles online: For more information, readers still have to go to the newsstand and buy a copy of the magazine.

E-zine only

There are already magazines that are only available on the Internet. You may have to pay a subscription fee to read the articles in these e-zines. It is predicted that in the future most magazines will only be available online. Is this what we really want? Reading a magazine on a computer screen may not have the same appeal as flicking through the pages while relaxing by the pool.

Would you rather read an e-zine or a paper copy of the magazine?

GLOSSARY

circulation	the number of magazines that are distributed and sold
current affairs	detailed reports on recent events and why they occurred
digital	computer-based; using an electronic signal that carries information using numbers
distributed	made available to people in different places
edited	when a text has been revised and corrected
editorial	an article giving an opinion
feature article	an in-depth article
freelance	not working for one company
genders	male and female
glossy	shiny
issue	a specific edition of a magazine
issues	problems or topics
layout	the design of a magazine page
online	available over the Internet
paparazzi	photographers who seek photos of celebrities
press releases	announcements sent to journalists to inform them about events or subjects, also called media releases
profiles	descriptions of people or groups
proofread	to check a text, looking for mistakes
quotes	the exact words said by a person who has been interviewed
review	to write an article giving an opinion about the quality of a product
subeditor	a person who corrects mistakes in articles before they are printed
subscription	an arrangement where the reader pays to receive a magazine in the mail regularly
target audience	the age group or sort of people the magazine aims to attract
trade	a type of skilled work, such as carpentry or printing
tripod	a three-legged stand that supports a camera

INDEX